THE
NBA
A HISTORY OF HOOPS

Published by Creative Education
P.O. Box 227, Mankato, Minnesota 56002
Creative Education is an imprint of The Creative Company
www.thecreativecompany.us

Design and production by Christine Vanderbeek
Art direction by Rita Marshall

Printed by Corporate Graphics in the United States of America

Photographs by Corbis (Bettmann, Steve Lipofsky), Dreamstime (Munktcu),
Getty Images (Andrew D. Bernstein/NBAE, Kim Blaxland, Nathaniel S.
Butler/NBAE, Focus on Sport, Jesse D. Garrabrant/NBAE, Barry
Gossage/NBAE, Walter Iooss Jr./NBAE, Neil Leifer/NBAE, Fernando
Medina/NBAE, Peter Read Miller/Sports Illustrated, NBA Photo Library/
NBAE, Dick Raphael/NBAE, Dick Raphael/Sports Illustrated, Jon
SooHoo/NBAE, SM/AIUEO, George Tiedemann/Sports Illustrated, John
G. Zimmerman/Time & Life Pictures), iStockphoto (Brandon Laufenberg)

Library of Congress Cataloging-in-Publication Data
Gilbert, Sara.
The story of the Philadelphia 76ers / by Sara Gilbert.
p. cm. — (The NBA: a history of hoops)
Includes index.
Summary: The history of the Philadelphia 76ers professional basketball team
from its start in 1946 to today, spotlighting the franchise's greatest players and
reliving its most dramatic moments.
ISBN 978-1-58341-957-1
1. Philadelphia 76ers (Basketball team)—History—Juvenile literature. I. Title.
GV885.52.P45G55 2010   796.323'64'0974811—dc22   2009034785

CPSIA: 120109 PO1093

First Edition
2 4 6 8 9 7 5 3 1

Page 3: Forward Elton Brand
Pages 4–5: Center Samuel Dalembert

THE STORY OF THE
PHILADELPHIA
76ERS

SARA GILBERT

CREATIVE ◐ EDUCATION

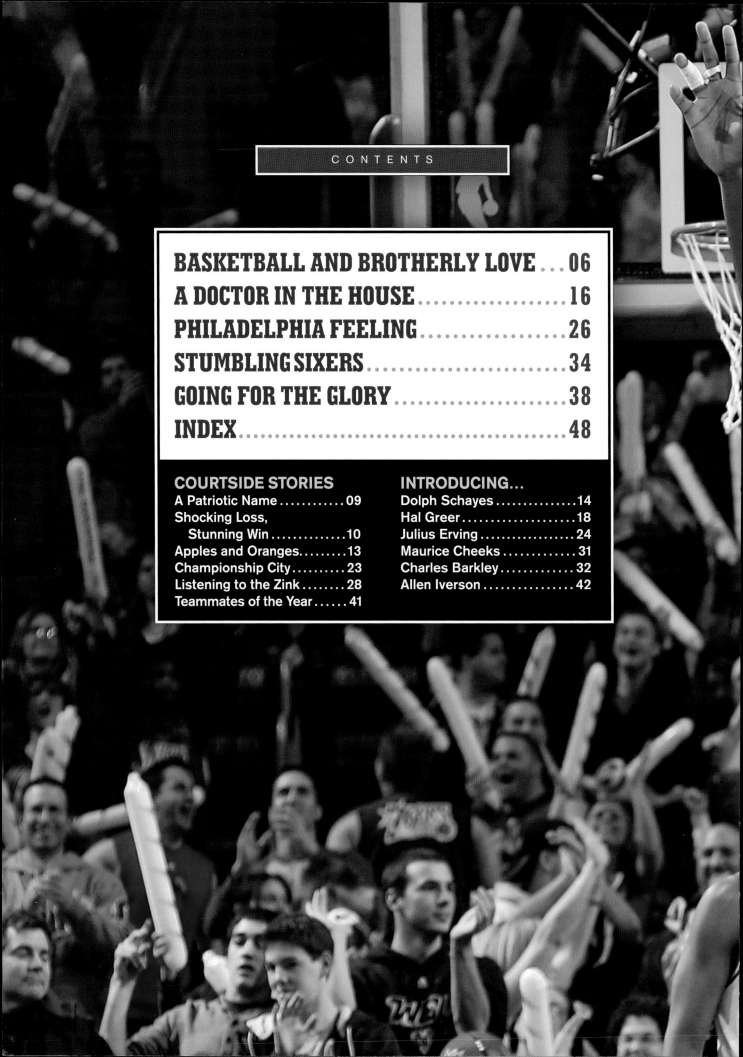

CONTENTS

CHAPTER ONE

BASKETBALL AND BROTHERLY LOVE

On July 4, 1776, delegates to the Second Continental Congress gathered in the city of Philadelphia, Pennsylvania, to sign the Declaration of Independence, officially forming the United States of America. That moment continues to define the City of Brotherly Love, as Philadelphia is known, more than two centuries later. Visitors come to see the cracked Liberty Bell that hangs in Independence Hall—the very building where the Declaration was signed. They also come to see the city's National Basketball Association (NBA) team, which was named the 76ers in honor of the city's historical significance.

The history of pro basketball in Philadelphia actually began with the Warriors, one of the original members of the Basketball Association of America (BAA), which was formed in 1946. The Warriors won the league's first championship, and when the BAA merged with another league in 1949 to form the NBA, the Philadelphia Warriors continued their winning ways. In 1956, they captured an NBA championship.

Commonly referred to as "Philly," Philadelphia is home to boisterous fans and championship-winning franchises in all four major professional sports.

B ut in 1962, the Warriors and their star player, center and Philadelphia native Wilt Chamberlain, moved west to San Francisco. Pennsylvania's diehard hoops fans were devastated. Then, in the spring of 1963, a pair of local businessmen bought the NBA's successful Syracuse Nationals franchise, which had been a perennial playoff contender for the past 14 seasons in New York. The new owners moved the team and its players—including two future Hall-of-Famers, guard Hal Greer and forward Dolph Schayes—to Philadelphia.

Guard Hal Greer led the Nationals-turned-76ers with his scrappy style of play, ranking yearly among the league leaders in steals and fouls.

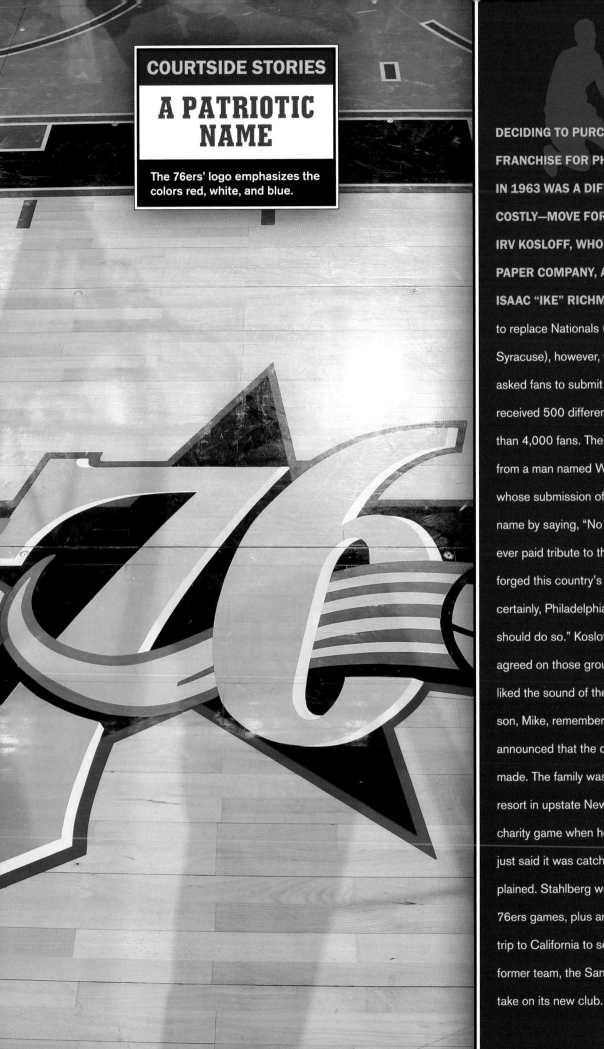

A PATRIOTIC NAME

The 76ers' logo emphasizes the colors red, white, and blue.

DECIDING TO PURCHASE AN NBA FRANCHISE FOR PHILADELPHIA IN 1963 WAS A DIFFICULT—AND COSTLY—MOVE FOR BUSINESSMAN IRV KOSLOFF, WHO OWNED A LARGE PAPER COMPANY, AND ATTORNEY ISAAC "IKE" RICHMAN. Picking a name to replace Nationals (its moniker in Syracuse), however, wasn't. The owners asked fans to submit suggestions and received 500 different ideas from more than 4,000 fans. Their favorite came from a man named Walter Stahlberg, whose submission of 76ers justified the name by saying, "No athletic team has ever paid tribute to the gallant men who forged this country's independence, and certainly, Philadelphia, shrine of liberty, should do so." Kosloff and Richman agreed on those grounds—but they also liked the sound of the name. Richman's son, Mike, remembered the day his dad announced that the decision had been made. The family was driving up to a resort in upstate New York for an NBA charity game when he told them. "He just said it was catchy and fast," Mike explained. Stahlberg won a lifetime pass to 76ers games, plus an all-expenses-paid trip to California to see Philadelphia's former team, the San Francisco Warriors, take on its new club.

ON DECEMBER 3, 1965, 76ERS CO-OWNER IKE RICHMAN WAS SITTING AT THE PRESS TABLE AT BOSTON GARDEN, NEXT TO THE PHILADELPHIA 76ERS BENCH.

The passionate owner was yelling at the referees one moment and then slumping over on the shoulder of a reporter sitting nearby the next. The team trainer and doctor raced to his side and tried to revive Richman as the game came to a halt and fans fell silent. Richman was placed on a gurney and carried quickly out of the arena, but at halftime, trainer Al Domenico returned to deliver the bad news. He walked into the 76ers locker room and quietly announced that Richman had died of a massive heart attack. Domenico made one request of the team: "If you never win another ballgame, win this one for Ike." And so, when the players returned to the court, they went on a scoring spree and won the game 119–103, their first victory ever in Boston. The following season, when the 76ers won their first NBA championship, center Wilt Chamberlain presented the game ball to Richman's widow.

COURTSIDE STORIES

SHOCKING LOSS, STUNNING WIN

Forward Chet Walker shoots over a Celtics defender in 1965.

When the Philadelphia 76ers opened the 1963–64 season, Schayes also filled in as coach, leading a veteran roster that included center John Kerr and guard Larry Costello. The transition was challenging for everyone, including Philadelphia fans. Even the much-anticipated November matchup between the 76ers and the San Francisco Warriors drew only about 5,800 people, and far fewer fans were in the seats for most other home games. The first season ended with a disappointing 34–46 record and a plea from owner Ike Richman for more local support. "We have a solid core of about 1,000 loyal fans," he says. "Next year, this should increase to about 2,500 for every game."

Richman did his part to entice those larger crowds by bringing hometown hero Wilt Chamberlain back to Philadelphia in 1965. "The Big Dipper" and Billy "The Kangaroo Kid" Cunningham, an aggressive rookie forward, gave Philadelphia fans plenty to cheer about. Under new coach Alex Hannum, the 76ers finished the 1966–67 season with a 68–13 record, the best mark in NBA history at the time.

The mighty 76ers breezed past the Cincinnati Royals and Boston Celtics in the first two rounds of the playoffs, then fittingly wrapped up

the NBA title by trouncing the Warriors in six games. "I honestly don't know when I've been happier," Hannum said. "This is the greatest team ever assembled."

That dominant team returned almost entirely intact for the following season and again won more than 60 games. Chamberlain, Greer, Cunningham, and speedy forward Chet Walker anchored a crew that led the league in field goals and free throws, averaging 122.6 points per game. But in the 1968 playoffs, the 76ers met an even greater team: the Boston Celtics, led by intimidating center Bill Russell.

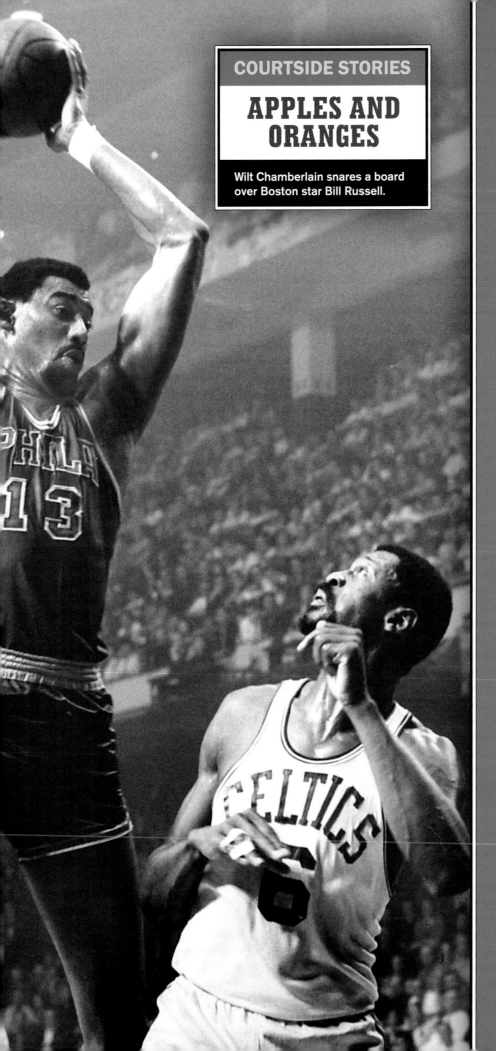

APPLES AND ORANGES

Wilt Chamberlain snares a board over Boston star Bill Russell.

WHEN THE 76ERS WON THE 1967 NBA TITLE, THE GOVERNOR OF PENNSYLVANIA SENT THE TEAM A CONGRATULATORY TELEGRAM. Governor Raymond P. Shafer had been able to celebrate with the team in person when the 76ers topped the Boston Celtics in the Eastern Conference finals, but he had to send his best wishes after the NBA Finals. "You have proved that you are the real champions," Shafer wrote. "All of Pennsylvania is proud." Then Shafer sent another telegram, this one all the way out to California. Before the Finals series between the 76ers and the San Francisco Warriors had started, Shafer and California governor Ronald Reagan (who would go on to become U.S. president in 1981) had initiated a friendly wager: If the Warriors won, Shafer would send a bushel of Pennsylvania apples to Reagan; if the 76ers won, however, Reagan would ship a crate of California oranges to Shafer. So when the six-game series ended with Philadelphia on top, Shafer happily drafted a note to Reagan. "The greatest thirst quencher in the world— victory and oranges," he wrote. "Want to try again next year?"

DOLPH SCHAYES PLAYED IN A 76ERS UNIFORM FOR ONLY ONE SEASON. By the time the Syracuse Nationals moved to Philadelphia in 1963, Schayes had already logged 14 seasons with the team and was widely regarded as one of its biggest stars. But he never expected to enjoy such steady success. He signed a one-year contract with the Nationals to begin playing in 1949. "That one year," he admitted later, "turned into 16 years." Schayes was an old-school player, relying on a two-handed set shot to score the bulk of his 18,438 career points, even after the one-handed jump shot had become the most popular way to score. He was equally aggressive on offense and defense and was a sure shot at the free-throw line—qualities that helped garner him the opportunity to serve as player/coach during the team's first season in Philadelphia. After playing only 24 games in 1963–64, Schayes retired as a player but stayed on as the 76ers' coach for 2 more seasons. His son Danny also played in the NBA, retiring in 2000 after an 18-year career.

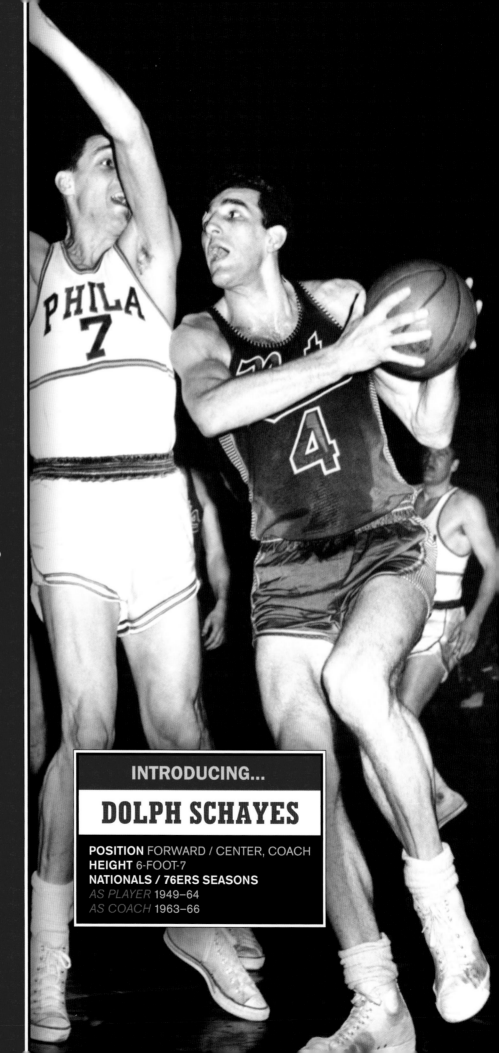

INTRODUCING...

DOLPH SCHAYES

POSITION FORWARD / CENTER, COACH
HEIGHT 6-FOOT-7
NATIONALS / 76ERS SEASONS
AS PLAYER 1949–64
AS COACH 1963–66

Although Philadelphia took a commanding three-games-to-one lead in the Eastern Division finals, the Celtics rallied to push the series to a deciding Game 7. Then, as the 76ers were down by two with only seconds remaining in the fourth quarter, Greer started racing down the court. Just as it looked as though Philadelphia might be able to tie the score, Boston's Hall of Fame forward John Havlicek picked off Greer's pass, and the Celtics won.

Alex Hannum coached the Nationals/76ers for five seasons, suffering only one losing campaign and capturing one NBA championship.

CHAPTER TWO

A DOCTOR IN THE HOUSE

That disappointing defeat was just the tip of the iceberg for Philadelphia fans. During the off-season, Chamberlain was traded, and Coach Hannum resigned. The team then pinned its hopes on Cunningham, Greer, and Archie Clark, a fleet-footed guard who had come to Philadelphia in the Chamberlain trade.

Although the 76ers made it back to the playoffs each of the next three seasons, they were overmatched each time. When a dismal 30–52 record kept Philadelphia out of the playoffs for the first time in team history in 1972, no one thought that things could get much worse. But they did. The 76ers began the 1972–73 season with 15 straight losses and ended it with an unbelievable 9–73 record, the worst NBA record of all time. The local media mockingly referred to the team as the "9-and-73ers."

Fast and high-leaping, Billy Cunningham was at the peak of his NBA career in 1969–70, averaging 26.1 points and 13.6 rebounds per night.

HAL GREER PLAYED FOR THE
SAME FRANCHISE HIS ENTIRE
15-YEAR CAREER, FROM THE DAY
HE SIGNED WITH THE SYRACUSE
NATIONALS IN 1958 THROUGH THE
TEAM'S 1963 REINCARNATION AS
THE PHILADELPHIA 76ERS AND
FOR A DECADE AFTER THAT. He
gave the same sterling performance
year after year, averaging 19.2 points
per game and finishing his career with
21,586 points. His teammates were
both bigger and more boisterous than
he was, but Greer quietly earned the
respect of his peers, his opponents,
and Philadelphia fans. "If there were
an award given for a player who is
most respected by basketball insid-
ers while getting the minimum public
appreciation, Greer could win hands
down," wrote a sports reporter for the
Philadelphia *Herald Tribune* in the mid-
1960s. Greer garnered his fair share
of awards, including being named an
All-Star 10 times and earning All-Star
Game MVP honors in 1968. But what
mattered most to the Hall of Fame
guard was that fans remembered how
hard he played every day. "Consis-
tency," he said. "For me, that was the
thing.... I would like to be remembered
as a great, consistent player."

INTRODUCING...

HAL GREER

POSITION GUARD / FORWARD
HEIGHT 6-FOOT-2
NATIONALS / 76ERS SEASONS
1963–73

N ow Philadelphia had nowhere to go but up. Guard Fred Carter
and forward Tom Van Arsdale paired up to lead the 76ers back to
respectability with a 25–57 record in 1973–74 and an even better
34–48 mark the next season. Although neither effort was good enough
to return the team to the playoffs, the 76ers finally had some momen-
tum in their favor again.

The pace picked up for the 76ers in the summer of 1975, when
the team signed brawny forward George McGinnis, who had been
named the Most Valuable Player (MVP) of the American Basketball
Association (ABA) the previous year. In 1975–76, McGinnis and his reli-
able one-handed jump shot helped the team return to the playoffs after
a four-year absence.

Philadelphia's recovery was complete when new owner Fitz Eugene
Dixon spent $6 million to obtain forward Julius "Dr. J" Erving, formerly
with the New York Nets. Erving was both an incredible athlete and an
entertaining performer whose amazing fakes and soaring dunks thrilled
fans. His arrival pleased his fellow players as well. "When I heard that
Doc was coming, I just fell down to my knees and cried," said Philadelphia center Caldwell Jones. "At least I don't have to worry about him
going to the hoop on me."

rving sparked the surging 76ers to the Eastern Conference crown in 1976–77. He and McGinnis combined to average more than 40 points per game during the regular season and were expected to power through the playoffs as well. Although Philadelphia made it all the way to the NBA Finals, the Portland Trail Blazers dashed its championship dreams in six games.

Cunningham, who had retired after the 1976 season, returned as coach in 1977. He didn't try to rein in Erving's highflying flair or the enthusiasm of burly center Darryl Dawkins, a colorful character who bestowed names on each of his colossal dunks—but Cunningham did appreciate the unselfish play of forward Bobby Jones and the quiet strength of guard Maurice "Mo" Cheeks, who joined the team in 1978. After having enjoyed a successful run in the previous postseason, the 76ers were disappointingly eliminated by the San Antonio Spurs in the second round of the 1979 playoffs.

A 6-foot-9 forward with a superb shooting touch, Bobby Jones quietly earned a reputation as one of basketball's most versatile players.

The 76ers were the underdogs in the next year's playoffs, upsetting star forward Larry Bird and his Boston Celtics in the conference finals and going on to face the Los Angeles Lakers in the NBA Finals. Dr. J and Dawkins fought hard against their star counterparts—Lakers guard Magic Johnson and center Kareem Abdul-Jabbar—but the Lakers rode Johnson's 42-point effort to a series-ending win in Game 6. "Magic was outstanding," conceded 76ers guard Doug Collins. "I knew he was good, but I never realized he was this great."

CHAMPIONSHIP CITY

Darryl Dawkins elevates for a shot in the 1980 NBA Finals.

WHEN THE PHILADELPHIA 76ERS SQUARED OFF AGAINST THE LOS ANGELES LAKERS IN THE 1980 NBA FINALS, THEY STARTED A CITYWIDE TREND. In the next nine months, three of the city's other professional sports teams would play for their respective league's championship. Only one of those teams, however, would actually win. The 76ers lost in six games to the Lakers. Eight days later, the National Hockey League's Philadelphia Flyers fell to the New York Islanders in Game 6 of the Stanley Cup Finals. And in January 1981, Philadelphia's National Football League franchise, the Eagles, lost Super Bowl XV to the Oakland Raiders. Only Major League Baseball's Philadelphia Phillies saved the city from a four-way championship shutout. The Phillies won their first World Series in October, capturing the title with a Game 6 win over the Kansas City Royals at Veterans Stadium in Philadelphia. "Everybody said we couldn't win," Phillies shortstop Larry Bowa said after the victory. "The Phillies aren't good enough. They don't have the heart, they don't have the character. We have all of the above."

PEOPLE NOTICED JULIUS ERVING'S HANDS FIRST.

"Dr. J" wore size 11 gloves—the largest made—and needed a size 13½ ring made when the 76ers won an NBA championship in 1983. Those huge hands helped him control the basketball with an ease that other players both admired and coveted. He was palming the ball by the time he was in seventh grade, about the same time he started using his powerful legs and long arms to throw dunks through the hoop. "I guess I consider my hands my best physical attribute," he said early in his career. "But I don't like to forget my legs either." No one could forget those legs; Erving's highflying dunks thrilled fans. His 1983 "rock the baby" dunk, in which he rocked the ball gently before slinging it behind his head and jumping over Los Angeles Lakers guard Michael Cooper to slam it through the hoop, is considered one of the greatest dunks of all time. But Dr. J's skills went far beyond dunking. He scored 30,026 points in his professional career, the fifth-highest in the history of professional basketball as of 2010.

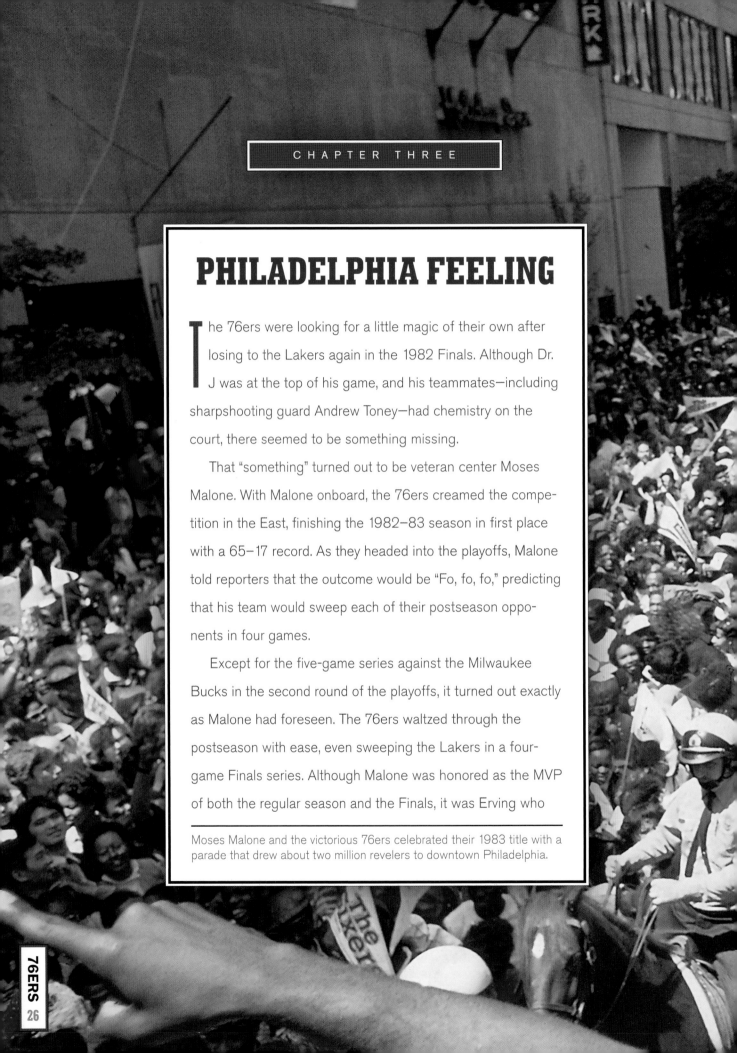

CHAPTER THREE

PHILADELPHIA FEELING

The 76ers were looking for a little magic of their own after losing to the Lakers again in the 1982 Finals. Although Dr. J was at the top of his game, and his teammates—including sharpshooting guard Andrew Toney—had chemistry on the court, there seemed to be something missing.

That "something" turned out to be veteran center Moses Malone. With Malone onboard, the 76ers creamed the competition in the East, finishing the 1982–83 season in first place with a 65–17 record. As they headed into the playoffs, Malone told reporters that the outcome would be "Fo, fo, fo," predicting that his team would sweep each of their postseason opponents in four games.

Except for the five-game series against the Milwaukee Bucks in the second round of the playoffs, it turned out exactly as Malone had foreseen. The 76ers waltzed through the postseason with ease, even sweeping the Lakers in a four-game Finals series. Although Malone was honored as the MVP of both the regular season and the Finals, it was Erving who

Moses Malone and the victorious 76ers celebrated their 1983 title with a parade that drew about two million revelers to downtown Philadelphia.

FROM THE 1940S THROUGH THE 1980S, PHILADELPHIA SPORTS FANS KNEW THAT NO MATTER HOW THEIR HOME TEAM PERFORMED ON ANY GIVEN DAY, THEY WOULD STILL BE ENTERTAINED. That's because public address announcer Dave "The Zink" Zinkoff—who worked at Philadelphia Phillies, Warriors, and 76ers games—always delivered a fabulous perform-ance. In his bold, nasally voice, he told fans that smoking was not permitted, but if anyone decided to light up, "please do not exhale." Zinkoff was best known for his animated introduc-tion of 76ers star forward Julius Erving: "Number 6, Julius, the Doctor, Errrrrrrrr-ving!" Fans also loved his classic call as the game wound down: "Twooo minutes left in this ballgame." The Zink's announcements were so memorable that even opposing players delighted in trying to imitate them. Zinkoff, whose career highlights included calling center Wilt Chamberlain's historic 100-point game with the Warriors in 1962, was also known for presenting congratula-tory salamis to players after particularly good performances. The Zink died on Christmas Day, 1985; on March 25, 1986, his microphone was retired by the 76ers.

COURTSIDE STORIES

LISTENING TO THE ZINK

"The Zink" announces a 76ers game in 1980, at the age of 70.

proudly hoisted the NBA championship trophy over his head while Philadelphia fans celebrated. "There was nothing pretty about what we did to the NBA this year," he said. "It was beautiful."

Virtually the same 76ers squad returned the following season but without the same results. Despite tallying 52 wins in 1983–84, the 76ers were beaten in a wild five-game, first-round playoff series against the upstart New Jersey Nets. Philadelphia would founder in the playoffs each of the next two seasons as well.

In 1984, some of the attention shifted from Dr. J to "Sir Charles"—forward Charles Barkley, a fierce competitor who was built more like a football player than a basketball star and who wasn't afraid to tangle with taller opponents. His youthful enthusiasm sparked the aging Sixers to a 58–24 record and wins in the first two rounds of the playoffs. But when Philadelphia faced Boston in the conference finals, the 76ers' postseason ended abruptly.

That was the beginning of the end. Injuries sidelined Toney for the entire 1985–86 season and hobbled Malone just before the team fell to the Bucks in the second round of the 1986 playoffs. Malone was traded during the off-season, and Toney's comeback was disappointing. Erving retired in 1987, and in 1988, Philadelphia missed the playoffs for the first time in 12 seasons.

Barkley had an incredible 1987–88 season, leading the league in scoring with 28.3 points per game and ranking sixth in rebounding. But even with the help of forward Cliff Robinson, he couldn't stop the 76ers' slide. The next season, the team brought in rookie guard Hersey Hawkins and swingman Ron Anderson, who teamed with Barkley to lead Philadelphia back to a winning record and a spot in the postseason. But when the 76ers met the New York Knicks in the first round, they were swept in three straight games.

Still, Philadelphia's prospects seemed to be improving. The team finished first in the Atlantic Division in 1990 and made a valiant run in the playoffs before falling to the surging Chicago Bulls in the second round of the playoffs. The 76ers returned to the playoffs again the next year but were stopped short of the conference finals.

Although Barkley remained among the league leaders in scoring and rebounding year in and year out, the forceful forward grew weary of Philadelphia's stumbling when it mattered most—in the playoffs. When the 76ers' 1991–92 season ended with a last-place finish, Barkley demanded to be traded. During the off-season, he was sent to the Phoenix Suns, where he promptly earned honors as the league's MVP.

STARS SURROUNDED MAURICE CHEEKS DURING HIS ENTIRE 11-YEAR TENURE WITH THE PHILADELPHIA 76ERS, AND HIS QUIET ACCOMPLISHMENTS WERE OFTEN OVERSHADOWED BY THE AMAZING ABILITIES OF TEAMMATES JULIUS ERVING, MOSES MALONE, AND CHARLES BARKLEY. But Cheeks's less-glamorous contributions helped the team win—and made him a favorite of Philadelphia's hardworking fans. Those fans appreciated his unselfish play almost as much as they appreciated how often he stole the ball from opposing players. When Cheeks retired from the NBA in 1993, he was the all-time leader in steals, having averaged more than two per game. "He would always steal at least one ball from me, every game," said Milwaukee Bucks guard Brian Winters. "As long as it was only one, I was happy." Cheeks himself was all about making people happy. He will forever be remembered for once rushing to the side of a 13-year-old girl singing the national anthem at a game in Portland, where he coached from 2001 to 2005. She had forgotten the words, and he ran out to help her finish. "That's just so Maurice," an old friend said later. "That's the essence of him."

INTRODUCING...

CHARLES BARKLEY

POSITION FORWARD
HEIGHT 6-FOOT-6
76ERS SEASONS 1984–92

WHEN CHARLES BARKLEY ENTERED THE NBA IN 1984, HE WAS SADDLED WITH AN UNFORTUNATE NICKNAME: "THE ROUND MOUND OF REBOUND," A REFERENCE TO HIS PORTLY STATURE AND SKILL AT GRABBING BOARDS. By the end of his rookie season, however, he was called "Sir Charles," in deference to his ruling over the court. "He plays everything," said former center Bill Walton. "There is nobody who does what Barkley does. He's a dominant rebounder, a dominant defensive player, a three-point shooter, a dribbler, a playmaker." Barkley's greatness as a player was rivaled only by his outrageous behavior and outspoken nature off the court. His controversial comments and impulsive actions (including once spitting at a heckling fan in New Jersey, only to have his spittle land on a little girl) often made headlines in the media. Barkley's behavior irritated 76ers ownership almost as much as the team's string of losing seasons bothered Barkley. When he asked for a trade in 1992, the 76ers sent the future Hall-of-Famer to Phoenix. Fans booed when he returned to play against Philadelphia the following season.

CHAPTER FOUR

STUMBLING SIXERS

Philadelphia did not fare well after Barkley's exit. Although they had picked up versatile guard Jeff Hornacek in the Barkley trade and drafted explosive forward Clarence Weatherspoon, the 76ers won a dismal 26 games in 1992–93. The team would be hard pressed to tally even that many victories during each of the next four seasons.

As the club struggled, Philadelphia kept trying to find the right combination of coaches and players. Before the 1993–94 season, the 76ers released several players, traded Hawkins to the Charlotte Hornets in exchange for point guard Dana Barros, and hired former guard Fred Carter as coach. They used the second pick of the 1993 NBA Draft to bring in 7-foot-6 center Shawn Bradley, who had just spent two years as a Mormon missionary in Australia. Then, midway through the season, Hornacek was traded to the Utah Jazz, and when the year ended with a lackluster 25–57 record, Carter was replaced by former Spurs coach John Lucas.

Despite the team's poor showing in the standings, there were some bright spots. Bradley was becoming a solid shot blocker, and Barros began earning a reputation as one of the

Although towering center Shawn Bradley was never a feared scorer, he could swat shots away like few other players in the game.

most dangerous point guards in the league. But injuries slowed the team's overall progress, leaving the 76ers to stagnate in sixth place in the Atlantic Division for two seasons in a row.

The revolving roster wreaked havoc during the 1995–96 season, when more than 20 players rotated on and off the court. Philadelphia finished at 18–64; only one team—the expansion Vancouver Grizzlies—had a worse record. The good news was that, because of all those losses, the 76ers "won" the right to pick first in the 1996 NBA Draft. They selected Georgetown University point guard Allen Iverson, who was known for his speed and agility while moving the ball up the court. "He's a special athlete and a special competitor, and he has leadership ability," general manager Brad Greenberg said on draft day. "He made it an easy decision."

The 76ers hoped that Iverson would live up to his nickname, "The Answer," and even as a rookie, Iverson did his part to help solve the team's problems. He racked up 4.1 rebounds, 7.5 assists, and 23.5 points per game in 1996–97, proving that he could break down opposing defenses better than anyone else in the league. "I try to put pressure on the defense," Iverson explained. "I am always, always looking to score, always looking to make something happen on the court."

Iverson and highflying swingman Jerry Stackhouse impressed the home crowds at the new CoreStates Center. The Iverson–Stackhouse

duo became one of the highest-scoring in the league, yet Philadelphia improved to only a 22–60 record in 1996–97. The team's final answer was to persuade longtime NBA coach Larry Brown to come to Philadelphia in 1997. Brown had played professionally in the 1960s and had been coaching, both at the professional and college levels, since 1972. He was recognized as a masterful teacher of the game—and the 76ers roster was full of young, inexperienced students.

But Brown did not stick with the same roster for long. By the end of the 1997–98 season, only five of the players he had started with still remained. Over the next two seasons, he continued to tinker, rebuilding the team around Iverson and hustling guard Eric Snow. At the end of the 1998–99 season, the 76ers returned to the playoffs for the first time since 1991. Philadelphia fans were so appreciative that they filled the arena with signs saying, "Allen Iverson for MVP" and "Larry Brown, Coach of the Year." The most prophetic, however, said, "We'll Be Back."

CHAPTER FIVE

GOING FOR THE GLORY

Although a thumb injury sidelined Iverson for 10 games the next season, the lightning-quick guard made up for lost time when he returned by leading the team in scoring for 22 straight games. With help from veteran forward Toni Kukoc, who recorded the team's first triple-double (double-digit tallies in 3 categories)—with 19 points, 10 rebounds, and 10 assists—in 5 years, Iverson took the team back to the playoffs in 2000.

The Indiana Pacers handed another loss to the 76ers in a six-game, second-round series. But both the team and its fans could see the potential that was building in this exuberant, young club. Team attendance records had been shattered during the course of the season, and many of those fans were confident that their patience was about to pay off.

They were right. In 2000–01, the 76ers opened with a decisive 101–72 victory over the New York Knicks, then went on to win their next nine games as well. Injuries slowed Snow and Iverson, but backup shooting guard Aaron McKie stepped up to cover for both of them and recorded back-to-back triple-doubles in the process. For his efforts, McKie was recognized

Allen Iverson was best known for his explosive scoring output, but his quickness also made him a sensational pickpocket on defense.

as the NBA's Sixth Man of the Year. More importantly, however, his team finished first in its division and then won three playoff series to surge to the NBA Finals.

The 76ers faced the heavily favored Lakers in the Finals but pulled off a stunning upset in Game 1. Iverson scored 48 points and quickly quieted the bold L.A. fans who had started shouting "Sweep!" as the game began. "I'm glad nobody bet their life on [a sweep], because they'd be dead by now," Iverson said. "Everyone said we can't do it, and that drives us." That drive, however, was overridden by the sheer talent of the Lakers, who won the next four games and took home the title.

Philadelphia lost its first five games the next season and put together a mediocre 43–39 record. Although the 76ers returned to the playoffs after each of the next two seasons, they lost in early rounds both times. Larry Brown abruptly left Philadelphia in May 2003, opting to take over as head coach of the Detroit Pistons, the very team that had eliminated the 76ers in the postseason just weeks earlier. In the transitional season that followed, two different coaches led the team, and Philadelphia struggled for wins, finishing out of playoff contention.

COURTSIDE STORIES

TEAMMATES OF THE YEAR

Aaron McKie looks to pass during the 2001 NBA Finals.

ALTHOUGH THE 2001 NBA FINALS DID NOT TURN OUT THE WAY PHILADELPHIA FANS HAD HOPED (THE 76ERS LOST TO THE LAKERS, FOUR GAMES TO ONE), THE TEAM STILL HAD PLENTY OF REASONS TO CELEBRATE. Members of that near-championship squad won four of the league's major individual honors, becoming the first team in NBA history to earn more than three of the annual awards. Guard Allen Iverson was named MVP, and Larry Brown was honored as Coach of the Year. Then shot-blocking center Dikembe Mutombo earned the Defensive Player of the Year trophy, and guard Aaron McKie was named the Sixth Man of the Year, an honor bestowed upon the best reserve player in the league. McKie, who had been asked to fill in for his MVP teammate several times during the season, was delighted that his contributions had been recognized. "I've never been a guy who's concerned about his numbers," McKie said. "The only thing that's important to me is to win. Whatever the team needs me to do to be successful, that's what I want to do."

INTRODUCING...

POSITION GUARD
HEIGHT 6 FEET
76ERS SEASONS 1996–2006, 2009–10

ALLEN
IVERSON

IN THE WORLD OF PROFESSIONAL BASKETBALL,
ALLEN IVERSON WAS CONSIDERED SMALL. But
what the 165-pound guard lacked in size, he more
than made up for in hustle and attitude. He was so
impressive during his first two seasons at Georgetown
University that Philadelphia drafted him with the first
overall pick in the 1996 NBA Draft. Although his heavily

tattooed body caught some 76ers fans off guard, his
confident play and aggressive gamesmanship were wel-
come catalysts to the slumping team. He was named
Rookie of the Year at the end of the 1996–97 season,
and four years later, he took home the league's MVP trophy and led his team to the NBA Finals. In the process
of attaining such honors, Iverson also gained recogni-

tion as one of the most prolific scorers in the game—a
fact that didn't surprise the young guard at all. "I believe
in my heart I'm the best player in the world," he said
after scoring 58 points in a game in 2002. "I'm just a
scorer." He scored 21,292 points for the 76ers before
being traded partway through the 2006–07 season. In
2009, he returned for a final season.

ixers management then started tweaking the roster again. The team

selected talented young forward Andre Iguodala in the 2004 Draft

and brought in veteran forward Chris Webber partway through the

2004–05 season. But early in 2006–07, Iverson called a meeting with

team management and issued an ultimatum: either find players to help

me win or trade me. Two weeks later, in mid-December, he was sent to

the Denver Nuggets in exchange for guard Andre Miller and forward Joe

Smith. Then, in January, the aging Webber was released.

The continuous upheaval took a heavy toll on the team. Philadelphia

missed the postseason two years in a row, and when the team finally

made it back in 2008, it was eliminated by the Pistons in the first round.

Before the next season, Philadelphia began to rebuild once again. The

76ers signed forward Elton Brand and brought in guards Royal Ivey and

Louis Williams, placing the future success of the team in their hands.

Iguodala ranked among the league leaders in steals and assists during

the 2008–09 season, helping carry the 76ers back to the playoffs and

becoming a fan favorite along the way. Iguodala could not take all the

credit, though. "It's that Philadelphia style of play," he said. "Everybody is

a hard worker. I think as a team we bring that to the table."

Andre Iguodala earned early renown with his dunks but soon displayed
amazing versatility as a scorer, passer, rebounder, and defender.

T he Philadelphia 76ers have enjoyed a long and proud history in the

NBA. Although it has not always been an easy journey, the team

has persevered and triumphed—just like the founding fathers who

gathered in the City of Brotherly Love to establish a country more than

200 years ago. And like those early Americans, the 76ers will continue

working to bring glory to their fine city.

Even though the 76ers struggled for wins in 2009–10, the stellar play of such youngsters as rangy forward Thaddeus Young (opposite) and swift guard Jrue Holiday (below) gave Philly fans reasons for optimism.

INDEX